Perfume Recipes That Will Suit Any Taste

Natural Recipes to Make Your Own DIY Perfume

BY

Jenny Kings

License Notes

No part of this Book can be reproduced in any form or by any means including print, electronic, scanning or photocopying unless prior permission is granted by the author.

All ideas, suggestions and guidelines mentioned here are written for informative purposes. While the author has taken every possible step to ensure accuracy, all readers are advised to follow information at their own risk. The author cannot be held responsible for personal and/or commercial damages in case of misinterpreting and misunderstanding any part of this Book

Table of Contents

Introduction

Are you ready to begin your perfume making journey? As soon as you make your first perfume, you will become addicted to it. This recipe book has proven recipes that always work. After you learn the basic secrets behind the process of making, you can proceed to prepare your own customized perfumes.

It is all about using the right essential oil blends. You have a wide range of scents from citrusy, fruity, earthy, and herbal scents. Don't think that essential oils have only a blossomy and girly scent. You can prepare men's perfume by using the right essential oil blends.

The best thing is that you have so many different options. You can prepare a solid perfume and apply it as usual. You can also make a body mist if you want the scent to be distributed equally to the whole body. Keep in mind that you have the best recipes in your hands, so you can find the ones that work for you.

Are you ready to start your perfume making journey? Let's go through the recipes!

Patchouli solid perfume

Solid perfumes have so many advantages. You can pack them in a small tin and bring them anywhere with you. You don't have to worry about the liquid limits when packing your solid perfume in your hand luggage. Here is a gentle and sophisticated perfume recipe that you can start with!

Time needed: 15 minutes

Yield: 1

Ingredients

- 2 tablespoons sweet almond oil
- 1 tablespoon and 1 teaspoon beeswax pellets, divided
- 20 drops orange essential oil
- 30 drops patchouli essential oil

Instructions

Take a small 2 oz tin. Add in the beeswax and oil, and set it on a baking sheet.

Put it in the oven to 200 degrees for about 5 minutes, or until the beeswax melts.

Remove it and add in the essential oil blend. Stir with a clean toothpick to combine everything. Close with the cap and let it cool before use.

Vanilla solid perfume

If you love decadent sweet scents, this one will amaze you. The vanilla scent is women's favorite, so that you will love this recipe. Apply the perfume on your wrists and pulsing points so that the scent will be spread as you walk around.

Time needed: 15 minutes

Yield: 3

Ingredients

- 4 teaspoons beeswax, melted
- 2 tablespoons jojoba oil
- 45 drops sweet orange essential oil
- 7 drops lime essential oil
- 2 drops cedarwood essential oil
- 3 drop ylang ylang essential oil
- 50 drops vanilla essential oil

Instructions

Melt the beeswax in a double boiler.

Add in the jojoba oil and mix well. Remove when fully incorporated.

Stir in the essential oils. Then, pour into small tins. The recipe will be enough for three tins.

Vanilla body spray

Body sprays are a must-have for the hot summer days. They will allow you to distribute the scent evenly on your body. This simple and easy perfume recipe will show you how to prepare your own vanilla body spray. You will save some money while also enjoy the process.

Time needed:5 minutes

Yield: 1

Ingredients

- ¼ cup vodka
- 2 drops ylang ylang
- 18 drops vanilla oleoresin

Instructions

Mix all of the **Ingredients** for our vanilla body spray.

Take a clean glass spray bottle and pour the spray in. Make sure that you shake before each use so that the oils get fully incorporated. Spray on skin or clothing.

Blood orange perfume

When buying a perfume is too stressful for you, you can always make it by yourself. Whether you want to save time or save money on shopping, you can check this simple recipe. It has a citrusy and sweet note, so that you will love this one.

Time needed:5 minutes

Yield: 1

Ingredients

- 4 oz fractionated coconut oil
- 5 drops lavender essential oil
- 17 drops blood orange essential oil
- 17 drops ylang-ylang essential oil

Instructions

Take a clean and empty perfume bottle. Add in the coconut oil, which will be your carrier oil.

Add in the essential oils one by one. Shake the bottle for half a minute so that the scents will be fully incorporated and diluted into the oil. Spray on the pulsing points.

Lavender Perfume sticks

When you think that solid perfumes are very convenient, you should check this awesome idea as well. There is nothing better than pouring it into a lip balm mold. When you want to apply perfume, you simply rub it on your skin, and you are done. This makes the process of applying easier and straightforward.

Time needed:30 minutes

Yield: 5

Ingredients

- 1/4 cup beeswax pastilles
- 1 tablespoon apricot kernel oil
- 2 tablespoons sweet almond oil
- 3/4 teaspoon lavender essential oil

Instructions

Start by melting the oils and beeswax. Create a double boiler by placing a smaller heatproof bowl into a pan with water. Warm the water to medium heat. Add the beeswax and oils into the bowl and melt them.

Remove perfume mixture from heat and add in the essential oil.

Pour into lip balm tubes and let them cool before you close the lid.

Long-lasting floral perfume

If you love feminine floral scents, this perfume will become your personal favorite. With only a few spritzes, you will smell heavenly for the whole day. The process will take no longer than 15 minutes, but you will have to wait for a day before using your perfume. Let's find out why!

Time needed:24 hours 15 minutes

Yield: 1

Ingredients

- 42 drops lavender essential oil
- 85 drops jasmine essential oil
- 85 drops sandalwood essential oil
- 42 drops bergamot essential oil
- ¼ teaspoon vegetable Glycerin
- 5 teaspoons isopropyl Alcohol
- ½ teaspoon distilled Water

Instructions

Add the essential oils in a perfume bottle. Shake gently to combine them.

In a mixing bowl, mix the water and glycerin. Add the mixture into the bottle.

Add in the alcohol to fill the bottle. Close the cap and mix it again.

Make sure that you leave it for a day. This will allow the scents to absorb, and your perfume will be ready in 24 hours.

Sunset summer perfume

Summertime requires you to switch to more citrusy scents. This perfume recipe will show you how to create the ultimate summer perfume that will be your top choice for the season. The combination of lime, orange, and grapefruit will bring the refreshing scent.

Time needed:24 hours 15 minutes

Yield: 1

Ingredients

- 77 drops geranium essential oil
- 54 drops lime essential oil
- 54 drops orange essential oil
- 18 drops cinnamon essential oil
- 51 drops grapefruit essential oil
- ¼ teaspoon vegetable Glycerin
- 5 teaspoons isopropyl Alcohol
- ½ teaspoon distilled Water

Instructions

Take a clean glass perfume bottle. With a small funnel, add in the essential oils.

Close the cap and roll the bottle gently to mix the essential oils together.

In a bowl aside, mix together the water and vegetable glycerin until fully incorporated.

With the funnel, add the water and glycerin mixture into the bottle. Close and mix again until fully incorporated. Add alcohol and mi again.

Leave the bottle to rest for about 24 hours. This will allow the oils to release the scent into the alcohol, and your perfume will be ready for use.

Endless sea perfume

If you are actually looking for a perfume recipe that has a sophisticated and light scent, then this essential oil blend will be your choice. The smells from spearmint, cedarwood, and bergamot are an excellent combination for a perfume. Making your perfume is so easy, and it will take you less than 15 minutes to do it.

Time needed:24 hours 15 minutes

Yield: 1

Ingredients

- 77 drops lavender essential oil
- 51 drops bergamot essential oil
- 51 drops vetiver essential oil
- 26 drops cedarwood essential oil
- 51 drops spearmint essential oil
- ¼ teaspoon vegetable Glycerin
- 5 teaspoons isopropyl Alcohol
- ½ teaspoon distilled Water

Instructions

First, pour all of the essential oils into a clean perfume bottle. Close the container and roll it gently in your hands to mix them.

In a bowl, add the distilled water and glycerin. Mix well until they are fully incorporated.

Remove the cap and add in the mixture. Mix again.

Add the alcohol in the bottle and mix it. Leave the perfume for 24 hours before you start to use it.

Natural men's cologne recipe

Men's cologne is a must-have. If you haven't thought of making it yourself, now is the right time to do it. This recipe will show you that making your cologne is too easy and straightforward.

Time needed:5 minutes

Yield: 1

Ingredients

- 4 drops frankincense essential oil
- 8 drops balsam Fir essential oil
- 18 drops orange essential oil
- 1 3/4 teaspoons 100 vodka

Instructions

Take a clean glass bottle. Preferably, use dark bottles, so that the essential oils aren't exposed to light.

Add in the essential oils. Pour in the alcohol, too, with the help of a funnel.

Close the cap and shake until combined.

Fresh citrus perfume

Perfume making is a great skill that you can master in no time. You really don't need to have any special skills at all. After you learn which are the carrier oils, you can experiment and come up with your own perfume recipe.

For making perfume, you can use pure grain alcohol or even vodka. It is crucial that you get alcohol that doesn't have any taste or color added.

Time needed:2 days 5 minutes

Yield: 1

Ingredients

- 1 tablespoon jojoba oil
- 2 tablespoons vodka
- 1 tablespoon distilled water
- 10 drops sweet orange essential oil
- 10 drops grapefruit essential oil
- 5 drops peppermint essential oil
- 5 drops lavender essential oil

Instructions

Add the jojoba oil in a glass container.

Add in the essential oils, one at a time.

Pour in distilled water using a funnel or a dropper.

Mix the perfume to combine everything together. Transfer to a dark glass bottle and let it sit for at least 48 hours. You can leave it up to 6 weeks if you want a strong smell.

Transfer to a pretty perfume spray bottle.

Botanical roll perfume

If you prefer oily roll-on perfumes, this recipe is the one for you. Add dry flowers before pouring the perfume for a nice decorative bottle. This specific mixture of essential oils will create a gentle and bloomy scent that you will love.

Time needed:15 minutes

Yield: 3

Ingredients

- 1 oz sweet almond oil
- 12 drops Lavender essential oil
- 12 drops Pine essential oil
- 14 drops Ylang Ylang essential oil
- 10 drops Orange essential oil
- Small flowers, dried

Instructions

Add small flowers into the empty roller bottles. The flowers are for decorative purposes, but you can omit them if you prefer clear bottles.

In a small mixing bowl, add the oils. Mix well until incorporated.

With a small dropper or a funnel, pour the perfume into the roller bottles. Add the rollerball and push it gently to get into its position.

Sophisticated earthy perfume

Bergamot and patchouli will bring all elegant and earthy scents to your perfume. This blend is the perfect pick if this is what you prefer. Transfer your DIY perfume to roller bottle or dropper bottle for an easy application.

Time needed: 2 days 5 minutes

Yield: 1

Ingredients

- 10 ml fractionated argan oil
- 2 drops neroli Essential Oil
- 2 drops bergamot Essential Oil
- 4 drops lavender Essential Oil
- 3 drops benzoin Essential Oil
- 1 drop patchouli Essential Oil

Instructions

Add the 5 types of essential oils one by one in the bottle using a dropper.

Fill with the carrier oil. You can substitute with jojoba oil, fractionated coconut oil if you prefer them.

Close the bottle and shake it well. Leave for at least 48 hours, as the scents will be released for a more potent perfume.

Everyday juniper perfume

This perfume recipe embraces the magic scent of juniper. The grapefruit scent will give it a kick of freshness, making this your favorite everyday perfume. When you are finished, you are advised to transfer the fragrance into a dark spray bottle. The dark glass will prevent the sunlight from altering the scent of your perfume.

Time needed:2 days 5 minutes.

Yield: 1

Ingredients

- 1/2 cup vodka
- 12 drops grapefruit essential oil
- 5 drops oakmoss essential oil
- 8 drops juniper essential oil

Instructions

Mix the oils and vodka in a clean mason jar. Shake well.

Leave the jar for at least 48 hours so that the scents will be released. You can leave it up to 6 weeks for a stronger scent.

Transfer to a dark bottle and apply it on your skin.

Bottled happiness perfume

Essential oils have so many benefits. By making your own perfume, you can use the benefits in the best way possible. This perfume recipe has a specific blend of essential oils that will give it a powerful scent.

Time needed:2 days 5 minutes.

Yield: 1

Ingredients

- 1/2 cup vodka
- 4 drops eucalyptus essential oil
- 8 drops grapefruit essential oil
- 6 drops juniper essential oil
- 4 drops oakmoss essential oil
- 2 drops cedar essential oil

Instructions

In a clean container, pour the essential oils. Add the alcohol.

Close the container and shake it well. The **Ingredients** should be well combined.

Leave it for at least two days for the scents to be released in the alcohol. Transfer into a spray bottle of your choice.

Rosemary and cedarwood perfume

Cedarwood is known for the strong woody smell that has a sweet note. When you add the refreshing herbal scent of rosemary, you get the perfect combo. These are the most used scents in the perfume industry, as they work quite well together. But the best thing is that it won't take you more than 5 minutes to prepare the perfume. Then, it would be best if you left it as long as you can for the scents to be released.

Time needed:2 days 5 minutes.

Yield: 1

Ingredients

- 1/2 cup vodka
- 12 drops eucalyptus essential oil
- 5 drops cedarwood essential oil
- 6 drops rosemary essential oil

Instructions

In a clean mason jar, pour all of the essential oils. Add in the vodka and close the lid.

Shake vigorously to combine the essential oils with the alcohol.

Leave it for at least two days before using it. You can leave it up to 6 weeks if you prefer a stronger scent.

Transfer to a dark spray bottle and use it as usual.

Lavender and lemon body spray

Nothing screams summer more than lemons. We love the sour fruity scent that brings an energetic feeling through summer. Now, you have the complete recipe that will show you how to prepare your own body spray. Let's get this started!

Time needed:5 minutes

Yield: 1

Ingredients

- 1 tablespoon vodka
- ½ cup boiled water
- 20 drops lemon essential oil
- 5 drops sandalwood essential oil
- 5 drops lavender essential oil

Instructions

Use a clean spray bottle for this recipe. Pour in the vodka and water. Make sure that the water is cool before you start.

Add in the essential oils.

Close the bottle and give it a nice shake. Spray all over your body while avoiding the skin exposed to the sun.

Vanilla and sandalwood solid perfume

Since solid perfumes are trendy, here is another excellent recipe. The spicy bergamot is lifted up by the citrus scent, while the sandalwood gives it a gentle woody touch. The shelf life of this perfume is about nine months.

Time needed:20 minutes

Yield: 4

Ingredients

- 4 tablespoons beeswax, grated
- 4 tablespoons sweet almond oil
- 30 drops sandalwood essential oil
- 30 drops vanilla oil
- 22 drops bergamot essential oil
- 27 drops grapefruit essential oil

Instructions

Create your own double boiler for melting by placing a heatproof container over a pan with water.

Heat to low and place the beeswax into the container. Stir until melted. Add the jojoba and mix well until incorporated.

Remove and add in the essential oils. Mix well again. Pour into tins and let it cool before using it.

Rose body spray without alcohol

Most of the perfume recipes use alcohol. It will help the essential oils dissolve and mix together. However, we know that some people don't like to apply alcohol on their skin. No matter what the reason is, keep in mind that you can always substitute alcohol.

Time needed:2 days 5 minutes

Yield: 1

Ingredients

- 2 tablespoons distilled water
- 6 drops lavender essential oil
- 15 drops rose essential oil
- 9 drops rose geranium essential oil

Instructions

Start with a clean spray bottle made of glass. Add in the essential oils one by one.

Shake the bottle gently to combine them.

Leave the closed bottle for 2 to 3 days.

After that, add in the distilled water. Close and shake gently to combine.

Perfumed baby powder

One great alternative to using liquid perfumes is perfumed baby powder. You still get to enjoy the pleasant scent on your skin, while preventing the skin from feeling sticky. It is an excellent alternative for the hot summer days.

Time needed:

Yield: 1

Ingredients

- 2 cups cornstarch
- 1 cotton ball
- 20 drops vanilla essential oil or any other scent that you prefer

Instructions

Add the vanilla essential oil over the cotton ball. You can use any other oil that you like.

Add the cotton ball into a large glass jar.

Add the cornstarch while leaving some space empty.

Shake it well. Place it in a dark place for three days. Shake two times a day.

When it is ready, transfer to a container of your choice. Apply with a puff all over the body on dry skin.

Fresh and energizing men's cologne

When synthetic and artificial fragrances aren't your thing, it is time for a change. There are a lot of men's cologne recipes, but this one will be your favorite. It has a carefully picked blend of strong herbal and woody scents that you will love.

Time needed:5 minutes

Yield: 1

Ingredients

- 8 drops peppermint essential oil
- 5 drops spearmint essential oil
- 5 drops vetiver essential oil
- 2 drops rosemary
- 2 teaspoons sweet almond oil
- 5 drops jojoba oil
- 5 drops vitamin E oil

Instructions

Take a clean and sterilized roller bottle.

Add in the essential oils and roll gently to mix them.

Add in the rest of the **Ingredients**. Close the rollerball and use it on your wrist and neck.

Strong perfume for him

If you're actually looking for an energizing and sophisticated men's perfume, this is your go-to. The citrus scent brings up the freshness, while the bergamot and cedarwood ground the perfume with a wooden note.

Time needed:10 minutes

Yield: 1

Ingredients

- 1 teaspoon vegetable glycerin
- 1 tablespoon vodka
- 1 tablespoon distilled water
- 16 drops grapefruit essential oil
- 8 drops vetiver essential oil
- 6 drops lemon essential oil
- 4 drops bergamot essential oil
- 6 drops cedarwood essential oil

Instructions

Take an empty glass bottle. Make sure that it is all clean and sterile before you start.

Add in the glycerin, vodka, and essential oils. Fill the rest with water.

Close the bottle and stir it gently.

Jasmin solid perfume

Jasmine is a very elegant and feminine scent. Jasmine essential oil can be more expensive when compared to other oils, so this is the ultimate pampering experience for you. The process of making is quite simple, and anyone will be able to do it.

Time needed: 15 minutes

Yield: 2

Ingredients

- 2 tablespoons beeswax
- 2 tablespoons almond oil
- 6 drops jasmine essential oil
- 2 drops vanilla essential oil
- 2 drops clove essential oil

Instructions

Melt the beeswax in your double boiler over low heat. When it is melted, mix in the almond oil.

Remove from heat, then stir in the essential oils. Mix well until incorporated.

When the mixture is still hot and runny, pour it into small tins or silicone molds. Wait for it to harden and apply your perfume as usual.

Energizing body mist

Body sprays are different when compared to perfumes. They are a diluted version of the fragrance so that you can distribute the scent on your body efficiently. The body mist has one secret ingredient: vegetable glycerin. This trick will keep the smell for longer, allowing you to smell like fresh citrus. The grapefruit and orange essential oils will give you a boost of energy to seize the day.

Time needed: 5 minutes

Yield: 1

Ingredients

- 2 oz distilled water
- 1 oz witch hazel
- 1oz vegetable glycerin
- 4 drops grapefruit essential oil
- 4 drops bergamot essential oil
- 4 drops orange essential oil

Instructions

Start with a clean glass spray bottle. Add in the essential oils.

Pour in the water, glycerin and witch hazel.

Close the bottle and give it a gentle shake. This will make the **Ingredients** combine and produce the signature scent.

Relaxing body mist

Lavender is known as being the best ingredient for relaxing. It is the perfect scent for the evening when you are preparing for bedtime. Spray this body mist all over your body after showering and head to your comfy bed for a good night's sleep.

Time needed: 5 minutes

Yield: 1

Ingredients

- 2 oz distilled water
- 1 oz witch hazel
- 1 oz vegetable glycerin
- 10 drops lavender essential oil
- 6 drops orange essential oil
- 4 drops bergamot essential oil

Instructions

Start with a clean and sterilized spray bottle.

Drop in the essential oils using a dropper.

Pour in the witch hazel, glycerin, and water using a small funnel. Close the spray bottle and shake gently to combine the scents. Use as a usual body mist.

Refreshing body mist

This body mist has a secret combination that will cool you down. This natural body mist is recommended for the exhausting and sweaty moments after a good workout. The tea tree oil has antibacterial properties, while the eucalyptus will give you a fresh feeling.

Time needed: 5 minutes

Yield: 1

Ingredients

- 2 oz distilled water
- 1 oz witch hazel
- 1 oz vegetable glycerin
- 6 drops eucalyptus essential oil
- 6 drops tea tree oil
- 6 drops peppermint essential oil

Instructions

Take a clean glass spray bottle to make your body mist. Add in the essential oils one by one with a dropper.

Pour in the rest of the liquids: witch hazel, water, and glycerin. Put the cap and gently shake the bottle to combine all of the **Ingredients**. Your mist is now done, and you can use it as you prefer.

Vanilla citrus body mist

If you prefer sweet dessert-like scents, then this one will become your personal favorite. Make sure that you use pure vanilla extract to get the best result. You can make a double batch and give these sweet body mists to your friends. You will be sure that they will love it.

Time needed:5 minutes

Yield: 1

Ingredients

- 2 oz distilled water
- 1 oz witch hazel
- 1 oz vegetable glycerin
- 15 drops orange essential oil
- ½ teaspoon vanilla extract

Instructions

Start preparing your vanilla citrus body mist by cleaning and sterilizing your glass spray bottle.

Add in the essential oil and vanilla extract.

Pour the witch hazel, glycerin, and water into the bottle. Close it and shake to combine the **Ingredients** together. Your body mist is now ready.

Exotic floral perfume

When we talk about perfumes, it is all about personal preference. This perfume recipe has the earthy and woody notes from bergamot and sandalwood that bring an elegant touch. The rose scent adds a floral scent that ladies love.

Time needed: 2 weeks 5 minutes

Yield: 1

Ingredients

- 1 tablespoon vodka
- 2 drops palmarosa essential oil
- 4 drops sandalwood essential oil
- 3 drops bergamot essential oil
- 3 drops rose absolute essential oil

Instructions

Start with a clean perfume bottle. Pour in the essential oils for your perfume.

Add the vodka. Close the cap and shake it gently. Leave the perfume for two weeks. This will let the essential oils blend well and release the scent.

Vanilla floral perfume

The floral fragrances are trendy women's choices. Blooms have a feminine and exotic scent, so no wonder they are essential **Ingredients** in fragrances. Pour it in a cute and decorative spray bottle. Your perfume is better than the most expensive store-bought ones.

Time needed: 2 weeks 5 minutes

Yield: 1

Ingredients

- 1/4 cup vodka
- 1/4 cup distilled water
- 5 drops musk oil
- 8 drops vanilla oil
- 8 drops helichrysum essential oil

Instructions

In a mixing bowl, add all of the oils.

Pour in the vodka and mix them well until incorporated.

Add the mixture in a spray bottle using a small funnel. Pour in the distilled water. Give it a gentle shake to combine everything.

Leave your DIY perfume for two weeks. This will allow the scents to mix and incorporate.

Bloomy spicy perfume

Anyone can make a good perfume with simple and easy to get **Ingredients**. Here is another great recipe that will replace the store-bought perfume. The combination of scents produces a feminine bloomy perfume with a spicy note from the clove essential oil.

Time needed: 2 days 5 minutes

Yield: 1

Ingredients

- 2 tablespoons sweet almond oil
- 2 ½ tablespoons distilled water
- 6 tablespoons vodka
- 9 drops lavender essential oil
- 6 drops cedarwood essential oil
- 15 drops clove essential oil

Instructions

Use a clean mason jar to prepare your perfume. Add in the sweet almond oil.

Add the essential oils with a dropper.

Pour in the vodka for your perfume.

Close the jar and give it a nice shake. Do this for a few minutes until the **Ingredients** are combined.

Leave the closed jar in a dark place for two days. After that, pour your perfume in a spray bottle.

Elegant rose perfume

Some prefer luxurious and sophisticated perfumes, while others prefer essential and plain scents. This perfume is for the ones that like a signature scent that is known for everyone. The rose perfume is suitable for ladies of any age, as it smells divine and classy. All you need are two **Ingredients** and 5 minutes of your spare time.

Time needed:2 weeks 5 minutes

Yield: 1

Ingredients

- 3 oz vodka

- 30 drops rose essential oil

Instructions

Use a clean mason jar to prepare your rose perfume. Add in the vodka and essential oil.

Close the lid and shake it well to mix the alcohol and oil.

Let it sit for two weeks for the rose scent to be released into the alcohol.

Strain with a coffee filter and a small funnel. Pour in a perfume bottle and enjoy your favorite rose scent.

Conclusion

Now when you have gone through all of the magnificent perfume recipes, you know that you can do it. We explained the whole process of preparing and the importance and role of each ingredient. You can choose to make some of these proven recipes as a beginner. When you practice and get enough experience, you will be ready to make your own perfume.

In this recipe book, you will come across lots of different recipes. There are body mists, cologne, perfume, solid perfume, and even a recipe for perfumed powder. You can choose the one that you prefer. If you don't like alcohol on your skin, we had so many alcohol-free recipes for you to try. Feel confident in yourself and start preparing your own perfumes. You can use them by yourself, or gift them to family and friends. They will certainly be amazed by your own fragrances.

New beginnings are always fun. Are you ready to begin this amusing journey? We guarantee that after this book, you will master your new hobby, save money on cosmetic products, and even expand your beauty business.

Author's Afterthoughts

Thank you for reading my book. Your feedback is important to me. It would be greatly appreciated if you could please take a moment to REVIEW this book on Amazon so that we could make our next version better

Thanks!

Jenny Kings